LET THERE BE LOVE

LET THERE BE LOVE

Sex and the Handicapped

GUNNEL ENBY

Translated from the Swedish by
Irène D. Morris

TAPLINGER PUBLISHING COMPANY
NEW YORK

First published in the United States in 1975 by
Taplinger Publishing Co., Inc.
New York, New York

First published in 1972 as
'Vi Måste Få Älska
by Bokförlaget Prisma

Library of Congress Catalog Card Number : 74–21696
ISBN 0–8008–4652–4

Contents

Preface

BY BARONESS MASHAM OF ILTON

Let There Be Love is a book written by an expert. It is only possible to write with such conviction and feeling as expressed here if one has lived through the experiences oneself. Mrs Enby knows what it is like to be institutionalized and she expresses very clearly that all people, wherever they live, have the same needs and dreams.

This book brings out the point that producers have left out in popular TV series such as *Ironside*, presumably in case they upset the audience, that disabled people do have sexual relationships. This does not apply to the play *Robert and Elizabeth*, which was a most romantic story about Elizabeth Barrett, but perhaps this was an exception to the rule.

I would agree very strongly with Mrs Enby that people with a disability are just ordinary people from a wide selection of the population, and that they remain the same people unless they are forced to spend too long in institutions. She states that life in hospital creates barriers between those inside and those outside—this is so, and it seems to be mainly due to the lack of privacy and the lack of opportunity for long-stay patients to have a satisfactory sex life.

This book illustrates very well that hospitals should not be places where disabled people just have to "exist". In my view, they should be places of treatment for ill people who either get better and go home, or die.

The statement that the world produces more and more handicapped people owing to accidents such as diving and traffic collisions is so true. I agree that more should be done to publicize accident prevention. This book helps to highlight the need for a change in attitudes towards disabled people. Even the very severely handicapped need to be able to preserve their identity and independence and must be allowed to feel free and unsupervised. How necessary it is to try and make the ordinary man in the street and the authorities aware of the fact that physically disabled people want to join in and live an active life in the community. In Britain we have more voluntary organizations working for the disabled groups which gives us an advantage over some European countries.

Children should be treated as boys and girls who one day will be men and women, perhaps fathers and mothers. It must be wrong for children to grow up as sexless people without an adult future. I also have come across schools which have refused to have physically disabled children in their classes.

This book is written by a Swedish lady about Swedish conditions; I think that in Britain we are more flexible in some of our rules, and more understanding towards disabled people in some respects, but I have found that basic feelings about people who are disabled do not differ much throughout the world. We in Britain are still behind some countries in monetary benefits and taxation relief for our disabled members of society.

Mrs Enby tells us disabled people are forbidden to adopt children in Sweden. Even though adoption laws in Britain are very strict, some physically handicapped people have become adoptive parents. I am happy to say my husband and I have two lovely adopted children, and I cannot imagine life without them now.

Like Mrs Enby, I feel there is a need for sex education

and counselling for those people who desire it. This should be available but not compulsory. Many questions may arise in someone's mind after serious injury. People should be able to discuss their sexual problems in a serious way, and it can be of great benefit to share them with someone in the same situation.

Mrs Enby points out a very real need—a place for a disabled person to go to in order to give the relative a short break, or to use in an emergency. This lack of emergency care is, I know, the most worrying aspect in the lives of our severely disabled people living in their own homes. The idea that those who look after their disabled relatives at home should unite so that they can project their needs is a good one.

The importance to the disabled of preserving their sexual faculties is illustrated in this book by the man who refused categorically to have an operation to relieve intense discomfort because he would lose the capacity to have an erection. It is true that it is no longer possible to draw up boundaries between those who are allowed to join in and those who are not. It is time for the sexual needs of everybody to be accepted, and I think this book will open the minds of many people. Accident or illness can come to us all.

Having spent nine months in hospital myself, I would like to join Mrs Enby when she says that one of the worst features of these hospitals is that there is nowhere for the patient to go with her or his friends. This is especially needed in long-stay hospitals.

It is good to read a book which says sex is beautiful, that it helps give the disabled self-confidence, a will to live and the power to go on fighting. As Mrs Enby says, it is important to love and be loved, to know that one is needed.

Masham of Ilton.

Sex and disablement

When people hear that I, who am paralysed and confined to a wheelchair, have a child, they often ask: "Did you have him before or after you became ill?" When I tell them that it was after, I know that they want to hear more. If we eventually become friends, the next question inevitably follows: "How do you and your husband actually manage?" People find it difficult to understand how I can function sexually, how I can satisfy my husband.

I so often come across questions about sexual matters that I am beginning to understand how difficult it must seem to a healthy person to identify with a physically handicapped person. People do not, as a rule, come into contact with the severely handicapped unless they themselves happen to be struck down by illness or accident, or have a sick friend or relative. Many have never given a thought to what it must be like to be physically different.

Women's magazines, films, articles and novels, commercially motivated, often present a false picture of the patiently-smiling, permanent invalid in bed, the grateful, disabled woman in her modern wheelchair. The image of the contented invalid seems to satisfy in the reader some need to feel sorry for someone less fortunate than himself without any obligation. The fact that people are constantly reminded that there are those worse off than themselves who are cheerful and courageous all the same, can be seen, I feel, as a link in the pacification of the whole of society.

Naturally people feel less inclined to make demands for themselves when confronted with pictures in newspapers and glossy magazines of happily-smiling, contented-looking physically handicapped people. But it certainly doesn't help them to identify with the institutionalized or to understand that they too are human beings made of flesh and blood, with the same needs and dreams as ordinary people.

Ironside, that most masculine of all figures in the popular TV series, differs from other famous detectives by not appearing to need a woman to love or to sleep with. The series seems to want to show that life need not necessarily come to an end because a person is confined to a wheelchair, but the possibility that Ironside could also need a relationship which might eventually express itself in sexual love has been left out. Perhaps the producers have deliberately designed the series like this in order not to upset all those in the audience who might find it unaesthetic or even revolting to watch a disabled person take part in a love scene. Not even those other well-known types, the popular criminal, the evil genius, the gangster leader in the wheelchair, who rule their empires with an iron fist, ever seem to need a woman.

The physically handicapped of fiction live their sexless lives either as angels or devils. How is it that this lie has been allowed to go unopposed for so many years? We are, after all, just ordinary people, a chance selection of the population, and on the whole we remain the same ordinary people even after we have become handicapped; ordinary, that is to say, as long as we are not forced to spend too long a time in institutions.

And yet, most people prefer not to think about our situation at all. Perhaps this general indifference is simply a question of ignorance. There is a widespread belief, even among otherwise well-informed and reasonable people, that to be handicapped enables a person to develop his soul, to leave behind all worldly joys and concentrate exclusively on spiritual matters as if the illness functioned as a catharsis through which the patient is cleansed and transformed into a new and shining being.

Nothing could be further from the truth. Of course, it is possible for a person to mature and develop after becoming disabled, but who is to say that this development would not have taken place just the same without the illness? You don't change into a different person because you are ill, you are not given some extraordinary, supernatural strength to bear your pain, and you don't suddenly stop thinking about sex. There is also the conflict between what you expected life as a handicapped person to be and the cold reality of what it actually is. The shining faith and the unselfish, humble gratitude somehow refuse to materialize. You discover that you really want everything to be as it was before you became ill. You don't want to be in an institution, you don't want to live according to a strict hospital routine, you don't want only to meet your loved ones during short, prearranged visiting hours.

Life in hospital creates barriers between those inside and those outside. The longing to be close is ever present. Sexual desires too. But how can two people function in the artificial, hostile world of an institution where not even a private guestroom or apartment exists offering privacy where closer relationships could be built up between the patient and friends, or perhaps where love and affection could develop between two inmates? For the handicapped too can love.

Hidden away

The world produces more and more handicapped people. The authorities calculate coldly how many dead and injured can be expected through traffic accidents and in industry. When you look at the figures, anybody who does not want to face up to the possibility of himself becoming disabled must surely be regarded as frighteningly naïve. There are already so many handicapped people that it is no longer possible to regard them as marginal. Severe and disabling injuries caused by car accidents, explosions or factory machines happen in an instant and hit the body harder than many diseases which as a rule take much longer to cause invalidity. There is no time to adjust to the reality of losing an arm or a leg or of becoming permanently paralysed. Suddenly you are one of the disabled, one of those with whom you have always carefully avoided identifying.

Why do people know so little about the lives and prospects of the handicapped? It seems incredible that most people remain totally ignorant about an existence which is not only our lot at the present moment, but is also the certain future of a foreseeable number of able-bodied people.

I believe this is because there is a limit to our capacity to relate. Some things are just too horrible to accept or understand. It is safer to dismiss that which troubles our consciences. We avoid it because if we don't, we would be forced to participate, to become involved—perhaps in personal sacrifices. To consider the blind, the totally paralysed, the desensitized in their hospital beds, the prisoner of the wheelchair in the lonely room without a lift, the deformed, the amputated, the crippled, requires a strength which we haven't got. We stop thinking about them, we turn away until, one day, we lie there ourselves with a broken neck, or we give birth to a spastic child. We have to find the strength then, we have to answer the questions: "What am I going to do? How will I cope?"

Not so long ago we hid our physically or mentally handicapped children or relatives in a room at the back of the house. We were ashamed of the sick and locked them away. The strong and the healthy must be spared the sight of the deformed and the crippled; those who did not fulfil the accepted norms had no right to join in. Nobody ever questioned these actions.

Today volumes are written on the subject of loneliness and nobody believes any longer that it is right to imprison those who are different. And yet, isn't this exactly what is happening before our very eyes? Society has largely taken over the role of the family as far as the handicapped are concerned, but not even society is prepared to accept them as anything else than a marginal problem. In spite of the fact that investigations have established the numbers of existing and future physically disabled persons, society is largely planned as if there were no handicapped at all in the country. Because the able-bodied, who can function as easily in an environment adapted to the physically disabled, do not remember the needs of the physically handicapped when they build our towns and communities, an unfair situation is created. Because our public transport, our schools, homes, pavements, etc., are made accessible only to those who can move freely, the life of the disabled is further restricted. It means that the strong and healthy decide where the physically disabled may live and function. Because only certain areas are made accessible, ghetto-like areas are created: here, they say, is where you will be allowed to live or work, here you can stay, here and here —but nowhere else!

Isn't this in a way the same principle as the one which prevailed seventy-five years ago when the physically disabled were locked away?

Homes and institutions

The difficulties the handicapped person has to wrestle with every time he tries to enter the world outside, be it for study, work or pleasure, are so enormous that it is much easier to stay at home. The result is a quiet, isolated, uneventful life, endless weekdays without meaning monotonously turning themselves into one long, miserably boring Sunday. Many physically disabled people thereafter prefer to spend their time in rehabilitation centres or holiday homes in order, at least, to have some contact with other people. These homes are often the only way out of a soul-destroying loneliness. But here too an unwritten law about the physically disabled having to keep themselves to themselves seems to operate: the homes are meant to provide relaxation and recreation and are always situated in peaceful countryside miles from busy city centres.

But what is the isolated, physically handicapped person supposed to rest from? As a rule he is not in a state of stress or exhaustion from hard, demanding work. The notion that the disabled are in need of a quiet and peaceful life is considered a mockery by those who with every fibre of their body long for something which will give meaning to their existence. Most disabled people, especially the young, do not want rest, but an active life.

In the homes, hospitals and institutions far away from

home towns and cities, where most of the facilities for pleasure, culture, work and education are to be found, the disabled lose all contact with friends and relatives. They are prevented in many ways from developing new relationships outside the limited circle of their fellow-disabled or the nursing staff in the homes. They become even more isolated than before. They feel abandoned and lost. And the rest of the world outside is also losing opportunities for meeting disabled people.

The very fact that so few people have any contact with the physically disabled is probably one of the reasons why they feel so alienated when they do meet them. Many are probably of the honest opinion that the handicapped themselves wish to keep away. It is not unusual to meet people who are surprised to find a physically disabled person who is neither silent nor modestly withdrawn. People feel alienated by the phenomenon of paralysis, they look upon it as something frightening, horrible and revolting, and often believe that the afflicted themselves feel the same.

Why should good looks matter?

I think that people find it especially difficult to identify with those whom they fear to resemble. Most people's experience of a physically handicapped person is often quite superficial. They see an unaesthetic body in a wheelchair, a twisted body dragging itself along on crutches, and they protect themselves against their fear by hurrying past and by thrusting aside all further thoughts on the subject. There is often no more contact than that; only a few get to know the real human being behind the defective exterior, an exterior which may not be acceptable according to norms with which we have all been indoctrinated.

These false values of the world cause suffering. The cult of the beautiful body increases the already existing inhibitions of the afflicted. I have met handicapped women whose dressing-tables have been covered with cosmetics. In a desperate attempt to reach the accepted norm of beauty, they spend hours on their faces trying out eyeshadow, mascara, scents and powder. We too want to be pretty and desirable and try to hide our crooked shoulders with surgical corsets and our matchstick legs with long skirts. Why can't people be accepted as they are? It ought to be possible somehow to stop this unworthy attention to appearance which is displayed by our Western society. Of course beauty is wonderful, but the world is full of non-beautiful people who also want to live and share the good things of life but who often withdraw in the knowledge that those who are whole would rather not look at their deformities.

I know of cases where severely handicapped people have been turned away from restaurants. I feel this is because of the fear of identification with the disabled and fear creates confusion and insecurity. I myself have always been treated extremely well when I have visited a restaurant or public place, but then I don't look particularly different although I am confined to a wheelchair. I don't suffer from spasms, I have no speech defects, I have reasonably good looks and I can eat by myself. Because I am married to a man with a good income I can afford to have clothes made for me which hide my physical shortcomings. I go to the hairdresser whenever I want to and I have many friends to go out with. But I am one of the lucky few. I belong to that group of disabled that people generally have begun to accept. Even amongst the handicapped, the better-looking ones are given preference. This I regard as grossly unfair. Are we really such delicate aesthetes that we can't tolerate a spastic at the next table in a restaurant who has difficulty in eating and slobbers and drips a bit? It could have been you—you are just lucky it isn't.

Why should intelligence make a difference?

If one isn't beautiful there is another chance of being accepted and tolerated as a handicapped person—namely if one is intelligent. Those in hospitals or institutions soon realize that if the medical authorities discover that they are intelligent, they will be given advantages over those with less-developed intellectual equipment. They are given a room of their own to study in, they are given opportunities to attend lectures and courses, they are provided with travelling expenses (which are otherwise reserved for those in employment), they are given quite different opportunities to meet new friends and they are held in higher esteem by the medical authorities, particularly if they are academics.

Before I started to read for an exam and was no more than an ordinary patient working away at some simple courses, I was not given any special attention by the medical staff. I was one of the girls in ward five at the rehabilitation centre. Nobody paid any attention to the fact that my parents had such a small flat I had to share a room with my father and brother when I was sent home after a period of rehabilitation. But when I passed my A-levels with distinction and I was mentioned in the newspaper and on the radio, conditions changed drastically. A larger flat was secured for my parents. The intelligent girl was to have a room of her own in which to carry on her studies; I was given a generous grant and my whole life was suddenly transformed.

I am always given a private room in hospital these days. The doctors no longer talk above my head but actually TO me. It is nice to discuss topics of mutual interest with a doctor—I only wish that other patients who have no particular academic background could likewise be allowed to talk over their problems with the doctor while he does his round.

I am thinking in particular of R., a girl in her twenties who, despite a severe physical handicap, works part-time as a telephone operator. She is forced to live in a geriatric home as she is unable to manage on her own and has no family to help her. R. has no room of her own. She had to share a room for many years with a woman in her seventies who was ill and tired and didn't want either light or sound in the evenings. R. requested a room of her own. It was refused. She asked if she could have a television in her room. She was told by the doctor in charge that as she was living in an old-people's home, she must realize that consideration for the old came first. It is obvious that the interests of the old must come first in a geriatric home— that the more seriously ill patients and those with a higher social status are given private rooms is another story—but young or middle-aged people whose interests and needs are quite different from the old ought surely not to be there in the first place.

I can't refrain from asking myself : would R. have been forced to share a room with the old woman if she had been working for a degree course? Would the authorities have let her stay in the loneliness, silence and darkness of the shared room if she had had a part-time academic job? I don't believe they would.

Perhaps it isn't so remarkable that the doctor is more understanding towards the academic invalids. It is obviously easier for him to identify with them—after all, he is an academic himself.

Purification through suffering?

I recently listened with horror to a preacher taking a Sunday service on the wireless; his theme was : "Arise, take up your bed and walk". I had doubted for a long time that there were people who still believed that suffering is useful. But I have since discovered that this belief flourishes among people who attend church. "The people who have suffered most," this clergyman was saying, "are always the most grateful. The room with the wheelchair can become the first step towards paradise."

Pronouncements like these have been made for centuries in sermons about Jesus healing the sick, Job being tested and the interceding power of the sick. The idea advocated by the church that illness has a divine purpose which can help to purify mankind does great harm to the handicapped in their struggle to be accepted simply as ordinary people who need more help. The Christian indoctrination turns us into a specially chosen people whose suffering has been caused by divine power. This belief seems to make it less important to create easier conditions for the disabled.

I remember an incident in an institution in the Swedish midlands when we were all ordered into the large assembly hall to listen to a choir and a sermon from one of the free churches. The preacher's subject was our illness, which he said we had inherited because of the sins of our fore-fathers. The whole hall was filled to capacity with young people in wheelchairs or on crutches. We were exhorted to mend our ways so that God in His mercy would cure us.

Some people are prevented from helping by the odd idea that sick people can be cured through faith; if this possibility exists, the argument goes, if the handicapped are able to help themselves, why fall back on the taxpayer? I believe this attitude makes it harder for people to identify with and understand the conditions of our lives, and actually adds to our unnecessary sufferings.

3

What we need is understanding

More and more people are being forced through accidents to relatives or friends to overcome their ignorance and lack of understanding of the disabled person's situation. A change of attitude is easiest for those who are faced with the reality of having to tackle the problems involved in living or associating with a handicapped person. For the afflicted himself the road to acceptance may be long and difficult, involving emotional experiences of inferiority and constant struggles against his own prejudices about what life as a handicapped person ought to be.

How much easier it would be for people to adapt to the new life of disablement if they could only know something beforehand of what is involved. They would then know that the handicapped live exactly like ordinary people, that they shop in the same shops, have children at school, go to parent-teacher meetings and to the hairdresser, travel abroad, that they can manage fairly well outside the hospital as long as they are given a little extra help mornings and evenings and with their personal hygiene.

If it were possible for people to meet their handicapped neighbours in the lift, in the street, at the pre-natal clinic, in the sex shop or at church, the trauma surrounding the handicap, the crutches and wheelchairs, would be considerably lessened. It would make it easier to discover that this is a person just like oneself, going about his business. If the disabled lived more freely and openly among the rest of the world, it would also make for a greater sense of security for those not handicapped—they would know that were they ever to become disabled, they would not be forced to leave their familiar surroundings but could go on living almost as before.

Such a society is no mere utopian dream. It is simply a question of persuading the authorities to stop their costly and, for the patients, destructive plans for larger and better institutions. The habit of parking people who need assistance in institutions in the depths of the country or in isolated homes in towns should be stopped. If the physically handicapped person was allotted a flat for which he was allowed the usual rent deduction and a home help for mornings and evenings, depending on his needs, the cost would amount to far less than the cost of keeping him in hospital. I feel this saving would be acceptable to everybody, not to mention the personal gain for the patient, who, instead of feeling like a parcel in the left-luggage department of the hospital for life—Number Five in Ward Two—would be allowed to be a human being and retain his own identity.

The disabled person easily becomes lonely when he is finally let out to live on his own after having spent many years in an institution. Old friends are gone and it is not very easy to make new ones. The surroundings may also be too difficult for the disabled person to manage on his own, he may not be able to go out shopping, to take a walk in the wheelchair, or go to a cinema. He is locked up once more, the only difference being that he no longer has to be obedient to strict hospital rules.

The all-round society

When the old beliefs in institutions are one day abandoned and the disabled are allowed to take their place in society, an effort must be made to keep that which was good and positive in the institutions—the adapted facilities, the sense of safety and security, medical attention, etc. It is not just enough to put a disabled person into a purpose-built home adapted to his needs, while the rest of his surroundings are suitable only for the able-bodied. The whole point of allowing a disabled person to live in society is surely that he should manage as much as possible on his own, that he should be able to go to the post office, the bank, the shops, the launderette, or a bar or restaurant. It may also be necessary for him to travel by underground or bus, which means that public transport must be adapted to suit everybody. It would probably be cheaper, in the long run, than an increased number of already costly travel allowances, and it would also save the authorities a great deal of expense if the disabled person was himself capable of performing many of the tasks now handled by the home help.

I live in the hope that the powers-that-be will build an "all-round" community where every member will be able to function properly, where builders who don't appreciate the fact that a purpose-built, handicap-orientated building is beneficial to everybody will no longer be granted permission to build. We are all going to grow old one day and find it difficult to walk up many flights of stairs; there are young mothers with prams who have special needs, there are all those who will one day, for some reason or other, actually join the ranks of the physically disabled. It would enable everybody in this all-round society to feel independent, to be responsible for their own actions, and to avoid having to live by proxy.

Every town and every community could provide a sheltered housing scheme, that is to say, purpose-built living units, flats or bungalows for the physically disabled. It is in the very nature of integration that the handicapped should not be removed to some special environment under the auspices of a charity organization, but instead should be allowed to live in suitably adapted homes wherever they choose. Physically handicapped people from the district could be housed in these living units, which would mean that they need not leave their familiar environment. The units could be built round a service centre which could easily be reached by telephone or an emergency bell. This way both the physically disabled person and his relatives, who may through circumstances be forced to leave him alone all day, would feel secure in the knowledge that help could easily be summoned. The centre could also provide a nurse for those in need of extra attention such as injections.

Obviously it is impossible for those severely disabled people who are in need of constant medical attention to move back into "life" in the same way, but more could surely be done to preserve their identity and independence. Even the physically handicapped person tied for life to her bed must be allowed to feel free and unsupervised.

It seems to me important to make both the ordinary man in the street and the authorities aware of the fact that the physically disabled want to join in and live an active life in the community, and that the changes necessary for this to happen are not only important to those of us who are already suffering from disablement, but could also be of use to themselves in the future. We can draw attention to our plight in a hopelessly impractical environment by asking people to give a hand with the wheelchair on to an inconveniently high pavement, or through an all-too-narrow door or lift—in other words, try and create public awareness of our needs.

People very quickly get used to associating with the physically disabled in streets and shops. This is one reason why I am convinced that those who hide away because they are ashamed of not looking like ordinary people do themselves and their good cause a real disservice. The more spastics or limbless people the average person sees, the less sensational it becomes. I know, of course, that for many physically handicapped people the struggle to get out and about is immense, but all the same, I feel sure that their numbers could increase. If physically handicapped youngsters, for instance, are seen often enough in discotheques, it will eventually be accepted as perfectly natural; exactly the same is true about physically disabled people living together and having children, joining clubs or travelling abroad on package tours.

Television can help

The idea that the physically handicapped want to keep themselves to themselves must be quashed. Television could perform a real service here by encouraging handicapped people to appear in various programmes, to take part in debates or be members of the audience. Not a mass exhibition of wheelchairs, as if all the inmates of an institution had suddenly been given leave at the same time, and not single shows where paralysis and all the horrors of physical disablement are paraded with almost obscene detail—which is bound to widen the already existing gulf between the sick and the able-bodied—but simply and naturally, one or two at a time at regular intervals until, in the end, it becomes so natural to have the physically disabled taking part in all kinds of programmes that they are no longer noticed.

Some programmes on the problems of a single disabled individual can have a negative effect, and can actually diminish both acceptance and understanding of the needs involved. All it often achieves is fame and glory for the reporter.

One of the people who really made me happy was a

well-known TV and radio producer. He has probably forgotten the incident, but when I rang him to ask if he could give me something to do and told him about my qualifications, that I was confined to a wheelchair and had already taken part in several programmes on the physically handicapped, he answered: "Yes, yes, but what else can you do?"

It seemed to me that his willingness to accept a physically disabled person as a potential contributor on merit alone, and not only in connection with the subject of disablement, showed real awareness of and insight into the disabled person's problems.

4

Physically handicapped children

In spite of the fact that I am myself confined to a wheel-chair, I am not going to attempt to describe what it is like to be a disabled child, or how the person who has been disabled since childhood sees himself as an adult. If you have had a healthy childhood as I have, you have shared so much of the healthy world that it would be a betrayal of those who have not had this privilege to attempt to interpret their sufferings and experiences.

On the other hand, what I do know about people who have become disabled as children is that they often display an ambivalent attitude towards sex. "That sort of thing is not for us," I have often heard them say, while at the same time confessing to a deep-rooted longing for a close relationship with another human being which only too clearly shows their sense of loneliness and isolation. Possibly they voice these anti-sexual views because they have identified themselves from an early age with the anti-sexual attitudes prevalent in hospitals and institutions where they have been forced to spend their childhood and youth. They were never allowed to play childish sex games, like other children, it didn't pay off to indulge in exploration; submission to the moral beliefs of the authorities was the safest policy —it would earn a gentle pat on the cheek, an encouraging word. Masturbation was regarded as wicked, discovery could lead to painful scenes. Acceptance of the prevailing opinion of the rest of the world that one was a failure as a sexual creature had, at least, the advantage of leaving one in peace.

I feel it is important for the physically handicapped to be regarded from childhood as sexual members of mankind, as boys and girls who one day will be men and women, perhaps fathers and mothers. It must be wrong for children to grow up as sexless people without an adult future.

"What are you going to be when you grow up, dear?"

"A lifetime patient."

Sick humour? Yes, but true all the same. For where is a child to go when he has finished school and has nowhere to live and cannot manage on his own in a disablement-hostile community? There is no room for love during long-term treatment, so the authorities adopt a strict and negative attitude from the beginning: "Don't touch yourself, dear. Nice girls don't do nasty things like that." "No" and "Don't" and "Wrong" and "Mustn't" . . .

Surely society could give enough financial aid to parents with physically handicapped children, including paid holidays, to enable them to have their children at home. In this way children would grow up in a normal home atmosphere with brothers and sisters and friends. The day when the doctor advised the mother not to breastfeed her baby but to hand it over to an institution straight after birth ought surely to belong to the past.

Protective attitudes

Many parents have an over-protective attitude towards their physically handicapped children, preventing them from becoming fully integrated into society. They want the child to experience a few happy, carefree years, unconscious of his or her handicap, they are terrified of the knowledge that soon enough the child will have to join the rest of the world and be teased and tormented by noisy, able-bodied children.

I think this is a rather dangerous outlook. It seems to me to hinder that child from establishing useful relationships and to impede his own future development. Why should the umbilical cord be cut later on physically disabled children than on healthy ones? Small children, as a rule, have no prejudices against those who are different from themselves and it seems a pity to wait for the confrontation until they have reached school age. It would be far easier to integrate the physically handicapped children in the community if the able-bodied children had already got used to their ways and looks from an early age. If we lived in a disablement-orientated society where wheelchairs could be used without difficulty, everybody would be used to disabled persons. There would be no need for parents to protect their children from life outside the home.

It would be of immense value if television, for instance, made it a habit to include physically handicapped children in their children's programmes. Children watching at home would learn at an early age that there are some who can't move in the same way as themselves, but who can join in and play all the same and be just as noisy as everyone else. It would be even better if the physically disabled children could also be integrated in playgrounds, boats, on the underground—anywhere, in other words, that healthy children are to be found. This would also give moral support to the parents of physically disabled children and perhaps even a few useful hints.

It must often be painful for parents to watch the failures and setbacks of their disabled child at school and at play; their wish to interfere, to smooth the way is only too easily understood. It would be naïve to believe that the transition from the days when physically handicapped children were kept locked away, to the freer, more liberal approach of today could ever take place easily and painlessly. But often much that might appear to be cruel or hostile turns out, on closer inspection, to be no more than healthy curiosity towards the physically disabled whose world has never before been encountered.

Exaggerated consideration

As I spend my own life in a wheelchair, I have never bothered to teach my son what so many parents seem to regard as important—that he must never stare at people who are different, people, for example, who sit in wheelchairs. He has not been taught that he must be particularly considerate towards physically disabled children. He treats them in exactly the same way as he treats his other friends. He is just naturally curious to know how they function.

A few years ago he happened to meet a thalidomide boy during a swimming lesson. He was interested to know how the boy, who instead of an arm only had a small stump growing straight out of the shoulder with a few fingers on one side, could manage, and why it was that he was born like that. He asked the sort of questions that the other children in the group would probably have liked to ask if they had dared, but who had presumably been told not to look at the "poor little boy" and therefore avoided all contact with him. They had been taught to regard the physically disabled as "special" people to whom they must not speak as to ordinary people.

There was a painful silence after Henrik's question. The teacher, who had no idea how to cope with the situation, loudly declared that it was a most improper question. The mother of the boy told Henrik that Charles was just as good as Henrik, that he was very brave in the water, etc. When Charles finally started to cry, the whole situation became so grotesquely out of proportion that a friend of mine who was there with her own child, in her anxiety to save the situation, called out: "Who are you to speak, Henrik, your own mother has to use a wheelchair."

Scenes like that are the sad consequences of an attempt at integration without any sort of preparation. It just doesn't work to bring a child along and let him mix with healthy children when the parents themselves are not capable of handling unexpected incidents. It doesn't work if parents give up the moment something happens which cuts them to the quick or upsets their good intentions. The children themselves must be left to cope with their own reactions. It is useless to sit around waiting for considerate, well-brought up children to arrive and offer to become friends and play with the physically handicapped child. Children just don't function that way. Little Charles was removed from the swimming class and Henrik was told he ought to be ashamed of himself.

I think it would be valuable if parents with physically disabled children could meet with adults who have been disabled from childhood. Discussion groups could be formed where the parents could ask the "experts" important and relevant questions and together attempt a solution of various problems. If parents could get to know adult disabled persons who live with the same illness as their own child, and who are perhaps married and have a family, it might help them to be less anxious about the suffering of their child. They will learn that the child has a future after all, that he can establish a real relationship with another human being. They need not worry too much that the child will be forced to live a life devoid of love or fulfilment. They may lose some of their own prejudices and taboos about sex and the handicapped and accept the normal sexual development of the child. It happens only too often that parents project their own negative attitude towards physical handicap and sex on to their children, with tragic results.

If Charles's mother had taken part in a discussion group she may have been better able to cope with the situation. She may have been able to explain that babies could be damaged by a tablet called Thalidomide while they were still inside the mother's body, that nobody knew about it until several malformed babies were born but that it no longer happened as the tablets had been forbidden, that she and Charles belonged to the unlucky ones but that it was nice for him, all the same, to be able to swim—and how would it be if Charles and Henrik were to meet again and get to know one another? At best Charles would have made a new contact and Henrik would have continued to mix with a physically handicapped child without all the paraphernalia of special considerations and prejudices.

Of course, children can be merciless, but they are above all curious and interested in anything unusual. I have come across this curiosity quite often in Henrik's friends. "Why are you sitting like that?" they often ask the first time they meet me. "Do your legs hurt?" And I tell them how I was attacked by polio (they are fascinated by the fact that the virus cannot be seen) and how I was completely paralysed and couldn't even breathe, but how I recovered so much that I can now drive this practical wheelchair. And I show them how to drive the chair and give them a ride round the flat or the garden, and they think it as exciting as watching Henrik's electric train.

I have discovered to my joy that it is easy for children to accept that some people do not function in the same way as others. There is no need whatever for me to withdraw when young friends arrive and imagine that I am sparing my child the agony of having a disabled mother. I just quietly show myself exactly as I am and the children accept it quite naturally. It is one way of making children realize that even the physically disabled can be mothers.

My husband always hugs me and Henrik when he returns from work even when Henrik's friends are around. They have never reacted against this as something unusual. I think it important for those of us who are physically handicapped parents to demonstrate that we are capable of living a normal married life in spite of our disabilities, and important, too, to show that society fails us as far as service, help and grants are concerned, especially while our children are small and we need them most; society also fails us in forbidding us to adopt children while agreeing that we are capable of bearing and rearing our own. This is not so in other countries where it is possible, though difficult, for the physically disabled to adopt children. The severity of the prospective parent's disability, his or her life expectancy, and a number of other factors are taken into account and each case is judged on its merits, though in a country such as Britain, for example, where the number of couples wishing to adopt far exceeds the number of homeless children, the physically disabled person's chances of success are not very good.

The school

If children associate with physically disabled children from an early age it will be easier for them later, should the occasion arise, to imagine living with a physically handicapped person, or to accept that a person, although disabled, could one day be the father or mother of their own child. I have unfortunately come across nursery and primary school teachers who refuse to have physically disabled children in their classes, but is it reasonable to accept this negative view? Is it reasonable to lock children up in institutions and give them special treatment because some people are so sensitive that they cannot bear to see them "suffer"? I feel we ought to give everyone a chance to get used to those who are different. There will always be different children. There will always be illness and accidents which cause invalidity—that much we know for certain. It would serve a humane purpose if we did our utmost to integrate the physically handicapped children into our schools and tried to create a broader tolerance among our children for those who are less attractive to look at. Why should they have to be hidden away and forced to go through mental agony because of their looks? Some of the Thalidomide children will soon be teenagers. Are they not to be given the same rights as other youngsters to develop sexual relationships? Are they to be kept away from discotheques and youth clubs because some "sensitive" people find it difficult to look at them?

It seems to me that the schools could play an important role in devoting a couple of hours to the problems of physical disablement, its most common causes, the dangers, for instance, of diving in shallow water, traffic and industrial accidents, drug and alcohol addiction, etc., and what to do in cases of serious accidents. It is equally important to inform the children of their legal rights, of financial losses sustained through injuries, the benefits and disablement grants available, and perhaps, at the same time, set them the task of working out what sort of living standard they can expect if they have to live on a disablement pension!

It would be highly desirable, too, for sex education to include unprejudiced and outspoken information on sex and the handicapped, with emphasis on the fact that the sexual impulse is a basic need present in everyone and that this need can be satisfied in many and various ways; that mechanical aids may be necessary where one or both partners are disabled and that no methods need to be regarded as wrong or wicked. Mention ought to be made,

25

too, that masturbation for those who are lonely and have no one to love is perfectly acceptable. This kind of un-prejudiced information is all the more important as so many young school leavers are going to devote themselves to the nursing professions.

If the State were to give the parents of physically dis-abled children more help and support, more children would be spared the anti-sexual brainwashing practised by hospitals and institutions.

5

To be young and disabled

I am glad I am no longer a teenager, glad that I no longer have to feel uncertain about the future or ask myself over and over again : will I ever get out of here?—or have to listen to the other girls in the ward whispering breathlessly about love and sex making my head spin with painful erotic dreams. Will I ever know what it feels like? Will I ever experience love—real love "which conquers all"—goodness knows I have read about it often enough!

We had a male student who worked as a nurse during the holidays in the baths of the hospital. We were all in love with him. We whispered about him at night. We were embarrassed when he lifted us out of the water with our hair wet and dripping about our faces. In a way he was our only chance. The only young man we saw in months. The male patients were kept at a distance, we caught a glimpse of them now and again in hospital corridors or at film shows in the large hall, where they were made to sit on one side and we girls on the other with the nursing staff in the middle—rather like it used to be at church in the old days.

It is nice to be thirty years old and no longer full of unspoken longings, to be married and have a child and to have left the most painful years behind. It is so easy to forget, to cross out what has been, to live on and be grateful that I am not the one who had to stay behind in the long-term hospital unit. But there are too many left, too many injured young people, too many children who have to grow up incarcerated in the narrow, impoverished world of the institution with its archaic laws and its own outdated code of morality. For their sake we will never forget, we lucky ones who no longer have anything to fear from the nursing staff. We will never forget what it felt like to be young and institutionalized; what it was like to be tucked up in bed on a summer afternoon when the sun shone brightly and it should have been good to be alive; how our hearts were torn with anguish and our minds one long scream of protest: here we are, forced to go to sleep at seven o'clock in the evening when young people everywhere are just preparing to go out for an evening's fun!

But there was nobody there to heed our protests, nobody trying to understand our anguish; communication is an uneconomical form of nursing and tranquillizers are cheaper to employ than staff.

We made soft teddy bears in occupational therapy and gave them away as mascots to our friends or kept them in our beds. We had our meals with our arms tied up in slings and we bought arsenals of women's magazines when the "shop" on wheels came round on Friday evenings. Once we were told that a famous pop star was coming round to sing for us. He never turned up, but the Baptists came and sang to us every month and on Sunday mornings the loudspeakers in the corridors were turned on so that we could hear the church services on the radio. We wore green-and-blue cotton jackets and cotton trousers, and on Sundays we gathered in a large hall on the ground floor crammed full of beds and wheelchairs for the visiting hours. The visitors would sit in little groups round the beds and whisper and eat chocolates. The flowers they had brought would stay, wrapped in their tissue paper, at the foot of the beds until they were removed and arranged by the staff in tall, narrow vases, not unlike those frequently used on graves in cemeteries.

And so, while life for the teenagers outside in the world goes on changing and they grow more conscious of their strength and worth, life for the teenagers confined within the walls of the institution creeps on with unspeakable, soul-destroying boredom. Misery and fear dominate, the young exist in the same conditions as the old : their physical needs, their dependence on help dictate where they must live.

More and more people are injured in traffic accidents, diving accidents, or work or at play. Most of those who are injured at work are young and inexperienced; they know nothing of hospital discipline and they end up in long-term units where the first commandment is silence and conformity. Occasionally there is a sensational report in the papers or in a woman's magazine or on TV. But for the most part there is silence. Nobody wants to know. It is taken for granted that things are for the best, hospital routine is accepted, relatives don't always have the strength to shoulder the whole responsibility—holidays are hard enough.

Routine is given a hasty facelift during inspection; patients are taken out, cleaned and combed and placed in chairs in the day-room. The inspector is invited to tea, matron herself serves it in pale blue china cups, the patients, too, are invited. They drink their tea from plastic mugs. The staff members smile and busy themselves with the patients. Everybody is pleased and grateful when the inspector, who is already longing to get away from the suffocating atmosphere, walks round shaking hands. The flowers in the windows, the clean tablecloths, the gleaming floors, the reproductions on the walls—it is all so friendly, so bright and cheerful.

But when the inspector has gone the pace quickens.

Supper is swiftly and efficiently dished out on disposable plates while stainless-steel washbasins and toothbrush mugs are quickly got ready. Everything has to be done within a time limit: feeding, washing, being turned on one side for the night, taking medicine, sleeping tablets, tranquillizers, having the light turned out—somebody grumbles a little although it is later than usual because of the inspection—five-thirty in the afternoon.

But there are others, young, physically disabled boys and girls who are slightly better off. They may have a job and a car, they may work on a degree course, be able to travel and have their own little purpose-built flat. Youngsters like that tend to keep together in gangs, perhaps because they often live near each other in specially allotted homes and are forced together by circumstances. They live in a world of their own. For some of them the world outside their own presents as many obstacles as it does for their less fortunate fellow-sufferers in hospitals. Their "cage" is only slightly larger.

A young man who had been a male nurse at a hostel for physically handicapped youngsters told me that there were some among the patients who had never been outside except to go to parks or on car trips. An eighteen-year-old girl had never been inside a shop, never been allowed to choose her own clothes. When time allowed, he would push their wheelchairs into a large store, let them look and choose, and take them to a bar for a beer or a Coca Cola. Simple, everyday things that mean nothing to the average person, become a feast and something precious to remember for those who are excluded.

I remember when I was staying in a home in the west of Sweden how we were all taken out in a bus once a month to a nearby town. The home, of course, was situated in the depths of the country in beautiful surroundings, but so secluded that it was quite impossible for any of us to get into town ourselves. We would all be driven to a large supermarket; one nurse to two wheelchairs. On one occasion some of us wanted to go to a small boutique where there was a sale on, but boutiques were not part of the plans.

This strangling of our initiatives has a most damaging effect. We don't always want to be thought of as members of a group, we want to be regarded and respected as individuals; we don't want somebody to do our thinking for us, we would rather make our own mistakes and learn from them.

"We who live in institutions are too inhibited ever to take the initiative and enter into discussions and voice our own opinions. This is a handicap we have for life . . ." writes a young girl in *Svensk Handikapptidning* (Swedish news for the handicapped).

"The first thing to remember when you are an institutionalized person," writes a forty-year-old man who has lived in an institution since his early youth, "is to be quiet and undemanding. You can voice your opinion but not about your own situation."

The patriarchal attitude is well established. Some of us once attempted to change this authoritarian rule by forming a small representative group consisting of two academics, a sailor and a typographer. One member of our group was an experienced trade unionist, we were among the oldest inhabitants in the home and our aim was to form a patients' association which would choose an ombudsman to represent us at conferences and voice our opinions on various topics, for instance the early bedtime, the drinking laws which forbade us to drink even a glass of beer or wine at parties, and all the restrictions against sexual contact of any kind. We felt very strongly that the staff ought not to devote so much of their time trying to prevent the patients from finding some sort of sexual happiness together. We felt that sex education and counselling on contraception and possible mechanical aids for the severely handicapped ought to be regarded as positive steps forward in a modern, humane society.

But during talks with the representatives of the hospital boards our suggestions were dismissed as so much nonsense and unpractical utopianism. They were not even prepared to consider allowing those young people who were capable of having sexual relationships freedom to do so. The principle was rigidly adhered to that those who were actually discovered indulging in sexual activity would immediately be sent home to their parents regardless of their parents' situation, and any later transfer to another institution would be left to the patient's local doctor. This principle was not to be altered under any circumstances. One of the reasons, some of the doctors insisted, was that it would be kinder to those patients who would never find a lover and therefore feel quite rejected. Although I myself had a private room, my husband was not allowed to spend the night with me but was given a guestroom in the attic which could only be reached by narrow, steep stairs.

In these institutions the authoritative rule is so deeply entrenched that there is no room left for discussions or meaningful talks between patients and doctors, only a few hasty words during the rounds. It is in a hostile atmosphere like this that many young people experience the awakening of the sexual drive and with it their need for a real relationship with another person, their longing for tenderness and love and understanding. But in a ward full of patients of one's own sex there are not many opportunities to fall in love—the doctor, the caretaker, one of the sisters or maids —a kind of love-hate relationship.

But sometimes it does happen that two people find each other, and then it becomes a question of winning the staff over to their side, of making the relationship appear as romantic and sweet as possible, of pleading with the staff nurse to be placed next to each other on outings, to be allowed a brief visit to each other's rooms or wards, or to be left alone for short moments. The whole ward rejoices when two patients become engaged—all is delightful and lovely. But if they should be found in an intimate sexual situation, the same laws are applied to them as to others.

The lonely ones who have no one to love are even frightened of satisfying themselves; to look at erotically stimulating books or pictures is something they dare do only furtively and in deepest secrecy. The positive and life-enhancing aspects of sexuality are never referred to at all.

Young disabled people are perfectly capable of having stable relationships with their contemporaries, but so often they are inhibited by the prevailing moral codes and taboos. They want a relationship but are afraid of the consequences, afraid of being parted from the loved one and placed in a more "suitable" institution, afraid of the cold disapproval with which they would be met if they were discovered.

"When you are a teenager and find yourself physically handicapped your friends come to see you quite often in the beginning while you are ill in hospital. They pat you on the back with words like : 'You'll soon be up and about and join in the gang again.' And you smile and nod and take a few deep pulls on the cigarette that hangs down towards the kidney-shaped bowl on your chest which acts as an ashtray. 'Eve is asking about you, you'd better hurry up and get out of here.'

"Fairly soon you understand that the old days are over, aeons of time have passed between you and the chaps after only six months in hospital. You get a feeling that you have to be perfectly well before you can be a member of the old gang again, or are they just being considerate? Anyway, they don't come quite so often any more. Finally, only one or two turn up. You talk about this and that, neutral things mostly, a bit of football, topical events, people you have known—a year ago—you ask about Eve, who doesn't ask about you any more. She has a new boyfriend, of course.

"Then there is leave. You go home and watch TV with Mum and Dad. You could have done that just the same in hospital. Mum has bought a lot of nice food and made your favourite dish for Sunday. Dad finds it difficult to talk to you, but then he always did. You ring up a couple of the chaps, but they are out of course, it's Saturday. Sunday evening you are back in hospital again. 'Did you enjoy it?' asks the sister. 'Oh, yes,' you say and try to look cheerful.

"Eventually you leave hospital. If both parents go out to work you are taken to a long-term institution, otherwise you go home—to a flat two flights up without a lift. There is a chance of moving to a ground-floor flat but Dad doesn't want to move. He was born here and his work is here. And Mum doesn't like to change her shopping centre. She has always shopped here and anyway, she is a member of a women's club in the district. She doesn't want to move either. You accept it. You read a little, do the football pools, go with the Hospital Friends to a football match now and again, or a cinema. But not very often."

For young people like the boy in the example above, the institution becomes his only chance of contacting people like himself. There are rehabilitation centres where patients go so that their families can have a rest or a holiday. Sometimes youngsters who are forced to stay in geriatric wards are sent to these centres in order to "get out" among their own contemporaries.

In institutions like these you live close together. Boys and girls live and eat and work together during the day and sleep on opposite sides of the corridor at night. The atmosphere is heavy with sexual excitement. Just to be able to talk affords a kind of satisfaction. For many of the young ones who have become handicapped at an early age sex is purely theoretical. They long to know what it is all about, they ache to try, to feel, to learn. But their desperate longing can express itself only in words.

They are all unknown to each other when they arrive from the towns and cities or from the lonely, underpopulated countryside. They talk about the parties they will go to when they get home again, about relationships they have had; they paint glowing pictures of the lives they led before they became ill and try to create an image of how they would like to be, how they would like to live.

And sometimes at night it happens that someone whose arms are strong and healthy silently moves her wheelchair into the room of her beloved and lies with him for a little while. It doesn't matter very much that they can't be alone—the boy in the next bed will understand.

6

To be married and physically disabled

He pulls open the door with a bang and rushes into his room and flings his satchel on the floor.

"Mummy, where are you?"

My seven-year-old boy is home from school. I am filled with a sudden joy and I leave my typewriter in the middle of a sentence and move out into the kitchen. In the hall the wheelchair makes a mess of the rug.

"Here I am, darling. How did it go today?"

He is sitting on the table eating cornflakes and milk. I haven't the heart to start fussing about table manners. Next to him on the table is his writing book. At the bottom of the page his teacher has put a large red star.

We talk for a while about the events of the day. He begs a little money from me, gives me a hurried kiss on the cheek and rushes out again.

"You have to be home at five," I call after him and move into my room again. In a little while I will put the potatoes on a low flame, lay the table, but I still have two free hours before anyone comes home. I put Vivaldi's flute concerto on the record-player and wait for the wonderful second movement. I suddenly feel like going to a cinema, a film by Bergman or Varda preferably.

I look around me, let my eyes take in the blue carpet under the white, low table, the bookcases, the little oil lamp, the flowering cactus. A beautiful home, but an existence full of anguish. In my heart fear crouches, ready to pounce.

My life depends on the strength of another person, I know I am living in the shadow of the long-term ward. For my husband freedom beckons through divorce the day he can no longer bear it. For me, unable to look after myself, it means a hospital ward full of people of all ages and various degrees of disablement, there are no other alternatives—I know, I have made enquiries.

But "love is patient, is kind, love does not claim its right," the Bible and the glossy magazines remind us. "For better or for worse, in sickness and in health," the church thunders. "You should have known what you were undertaking," the welfare officers say. In reality it doesn't work out like that even when two people love each other very much. The needs of the physically handicapped person will always be a strain on the able-bodied partner, they will restrict him and provoke in him a longing for freedom. In the evenings, at night and during holidays he is tied, he may have to get up at night and turn the patient over, look after the children, open or shut windows, he may feel exhausted in the morning before his day's work starts. A day out fishing, a week in the country on his own becomes a necessity.

I once asked a doctor to accept me in his hospital ward for a week so that my husband could continue his studies in peace and quiet.

"Mrs Enby," he said, "it would be cheaper to send you to a luxury hotel than to accept you in hospital. You and your husband have chosen to live together, you have to accept the consequences."

"And what happens if he hasn't the strength to carry on, if he leaves me?"

"That is a different thing. We will naturally help you if you are alone, find you a place in a hospital or a home for the disabled. But you must understand that you can't just come along and ask to be received when it suits you."

But we do want to stay together, we are a family unit. Only sometimes it happens that one grows too weary to go on and a rest and a change is badly needed. On paper the help provided by the State looks so humane and generous . . .

What strikes me as quite horrible is the fact that only the intelligent and persevering manage to penetrate the wall of resistance one comes up against when seeking lawful social benefits. Those who are not so intelligent or persevering are helped as little as possible. Many benefits are simply not mentioned, this is an open secret admitted even by the social workers themselves.

From what I have seen it looks to me as if many people who look after their physically disabled relatives at home are not given the understanding and appreciation of which they are worthy. Instead of being made to feel that they are performing an important role in society, they are treated with suspicion when they ask for assistance. They are sometimes treated as if they were anti-social, ready to grasp as many advantages for themselves as possible. My husband often says with a touch of irony that if he had not fallen in love with a handicapped girl, he would have been a "respected" member of society and not have had to suffer the humiliations meted out to him by the officials of the Welfare State. It seems more than unfair that so little is done for those who have the courage and strength to take on the burden of nursing their loved ones at home. Nor is it easy for the disabled person herself to watch her family and friends continually giving more than their strength allows, to see them perhaps lose opportunities and advancements in their careers with the all too minimal disablement grants and pensions as a poor compensation.

I sometimes feel like a clinging vine, I feel that I am selfishly holding on to the security that my marriage gives me. My tiny frightened ego clings to the safety and free-

dom of my own home. I have a husband, a child, a bedroom of my own—mine, mine, mine. The cold, cheerless
years in institutions have left their mark. In the depths of
my being a panic fear of one day having to return lives
on. Every day is borrowed time, it is like a precious,
longed-for holiday.

I move my wheelchair to the window. It is early evening, I put my arms on the windowsill and stretch up so
that I can look out at the street. The street lights are on,
a little rain is falling, making yellow pools appear in the
gutters. The lights are reflected in shop windows and cars.
I sit here eager as a hungry hawk looking for my husband's
car, ready to throw myself at him with questions and talk
the moment I hear his steps in the hall. I long for human
warmth and contact after a day without meaningful work.
He may be exhausted, worn out after a busy day.

To live by proxy, to consume passively what others have
to tell, to be nursed, fed and put to bed makes for an
uneven relationship. I know that marriage should consist
of two independent personalities, both able to make outside
contacts, both gaining self-confidence and stimulus from
independent work, income, friends. I once tried to talk
about this to a social research worker. "Why should you
worry about money?" he asked. "Your husband will soon
be a qualified doctor."

"I know, but what happens if I have a divorce?"

"I hope you won't be as stupid as that," he answered.

But to be married must mean much more than just
being economically safeguarded. Marriage should not consist of a provider and a receiver but of two equally independent persons. It is important that the physically disabled person be given sufficient economic support by the
State to live an independent life. The physically disabled
spouse ought to be able to break off an unhappy marriage
without the fear of ending up in a hospital ward or in

absolute isolation. Many go on enduring a marriage which has long since died because they have nowhere else to go. Without work, without the possibility of finding a suitable home, without income, they are helpless.

I would like to see all those who look after the old, the physically disabled and the sick at home organized into a united front, a platform from which they could fight for their rights: compensation, higher disablement grants, paid holidays and home assistance when they are too tired to carry on. The people who look after the sick at home are saving the country enormous sums of money each year and they also provide empty beds in the hospitals. Just imagine what would happen if all of them suddenly stopped taking care of their sick!

I would like to urge all those who intend to nurse a disabled relative at home, or who are considering living with a disabled boy or girl, to play their cards right. They have many trumps in their hands. If they look after the patient at home they are saving the community a large sum of money which gives them the right to demand help and technical assistance, there is no need for them to work until they drop.

There are short weekend holidays for tired husbands and wives at cheap prices. How wonderful it would be if something similar could be arranged for couples where one or both are handicapped, where staff who could help the disabled were available. Couples do not always want to be parted in order to find change and rest, it would be invaluable to their physical and mental health if they could go away together for a short while.

7

Sex and rehabilitation

The valuable part sex plays in successful rehabilitation seems to have been discovered only since scientific essays have been written on the subject. In reality one would have thought that all that was neeeded was a bit of common sense and plain understanding. As the importance of sexuality for the development of the personality, as advocated by Freud, has long since been accepted, it seems rather odd to believe that it affects all human beings except the physically handicapped, and even odder that the investigations which have been carried out on the subject of sex and the handicapped have had no influence whatever on the work of rehabilitation in Sweden.

Sexuality in its deepest meaning does not only concern the physical side culminating in the sexual act itself, but also all that is sensuous and beautiful, a man's self-confidence, his will to live, his power to go on fighting. It is important to love and be loved, to know that one is needed. It is when a man has enough faith in his own lovableness and his own ego that he is best equipped to face an emergency. But if this faith is taken away, if by ignoring or dismissing the sexual part of his personality he is made to believe that he is incapable of functioning sexually, the whole process of his rehabilitation is undermined.

When you find yourself suddenly physically injured you know, as a rule, very little about your own situation. You grow increasingly unsure of yourself and frightened of the future, you wonder if life will ever be the same as before and how—if you are sexually aware—you are going to function in bed again. As the physical changes in your injured body and the general attitude of your environment have already made you feel a sexual reject, you feel shy and embarrassed that your thoughts are constantly occupied with sex. You feel you are doing something forbidden and the conflict creates a state of anxiety. The will to take part in your own rehabilitation dwindles. Your fighting spirit all but disappears, you become passive during the physical exercises, your thoughts keep circling round your injured body. When some of your sensory nerves no longer function, when your legs are paralysed and your whole existence threatened, it is not very easy to enter wholeheartedly into the training programme: how to hold your fork, how to put on a stocking, how to move your wheelchair, etc.

Rehabilitation is surely more than physical training and occupational therapy. To prevent fears, inhibitions and anxieties from growing within the patient seems to me to be just as important, and it can't be achieved by teaching the patient to weave or paint. Nor do I feel that the cookery classes provided by some hospitals in purpose-built kitchens—good though they are—can be regarded as steps in the right direction on the road to recovery, nor visits to the hairdresser or short walks in the hospital grounds. The longer you are kept in an institution and trained and rehabilitated, the more difficult it is going to be to take part in real life outside. Life in the hospital becomes the real one, outside is the alien world to which you have once belonged but which you can think of now only as frightening. And when you finally rejoin it, it is easier to hide away, to stay in your purpose-built, ground-floor flat, or perhaps venture out for a drive, and from inside the safety of your car, propped up so that nobody can see that you are handicapped, you dare to put your sexual desirability to the test with a quiet little flirt.

The door to the outside world must remain open all the time the physically disabled person lives in hospital. He must not feel that he is acceptable only when he has improved physically; he belongs all the time to the world outside, that is the one he wants to become acclimatized to, not to the limited hospital world. That is why it is so important for the patient to meet "ordinary" people by going out shopping, or visiting restaurants while on crutches or in a wheelchair. That is the only way to get accustomed to people staring and asking questions, to grow used to having to ask for help on stairs and pavements. It is good training for the physically disabled to learn to function in everyday life and to acquire self-confidence which will prevent them from withdrawing into a stultifying shyness which immobilizes their will to recovery and their efforts towards integration. Sexuality is a natural part of this integration. The physically disabled are real men and women with real needs for personal relationships, love and sex.

But somehow it appears as if doctors regarded this part of the rehabilitation service as rather embarrassing and of less importance. What seems to me so horrible is that sex is not only disregarded but that efforts are made to actually prevent any kind of sexual activity among the patients. I should have thought that it would be regarded as progress when a physically handicapped person stops thinking of himself as a sexual failure and begins instead to devote himself to a life-enriching sexual relationship with another human being. All his rehabilitation prospects will improve. For isn't it true that we all use our sexuality to boost our ego? Don't we all like to imagine that if we wanted to, we could easily have a sexual relationship? I know many cases from my own stays in institutions where a little flirt between two patients has broken the boredom and hopelessness of their lives and strengthened their will to live. Sometimes they have managed to fight their way out of their isolation and they have created conditions which made it possible for them to share a life in the outside world. By pooling their resources of muscles and willpower, it has sometimes happened that even severely handicapped people have managed to cope on their own together.

Could it ever be regarded as anything but the most blatant interference in people's personal freedom when the hospital authorities brusquely stop a relationship of this sort and the partners are separated by hospital staff, or one of them is sent home to a lonely life without any possibility of ever meeting again?

Degrading experiences of this kind often create deep and long-lasting depressions in the physically disabled person. Interest in personal hygiene and looks diminishes and rehabilitation becomes meaningless.

I remember how lonely I felt when I had first contracted polio. My boyfriend wrote to me less and less often. I no longer thought it particularly important how I looked or what I wore. The only thing I really cared about was my long hair. The staff was supposed to give eight minutes every morning to each patient and it was difficult to keep to that limit while combing my long, dishevelled hair. I had difficulty breathing and I was afraid of being alone so the door between my room and the corridor was left open throughout the day and I could watch the staff hurrying past.

Another patient, a man about thirty-five years old who worked in the hospital workshop, used to nod to me as he passed my room. Sometimes he would stop and say a few words. I began to look forward to his visits and started to take an interest in my looks again. He called in every day and we chatted about this and that, about the hospital food and the weather. I wanted him to like me, it almost became a challenge. One day he kissed me on the cheek. I was thrilled. I could still make a man want me in spite of being a polio victim. I continued to wait for him every day, but he never returned.

One of the nurses who had seen him give me that gentle kiss on the cheek had reported it to the sister who instantly forbade him to visit me. I no longer wanted to live. I didn't want to eat, didn't want to practise sitting up in the wheel-chair and I let them cut my hair. My will to live and self-confidence had been crushed and it was a long time before I recovered. The reason I eventually took up my studies again and managed to pass my exams was because I found a husband who believed in me and encouraged me and made me feel needed and important.

How a person manages to live through his traumatic experience depends to a great extent on the support of the people around him. Even the most severely disabled need to be regarded as ordinary human beings, to feel liked and appreciated. A flirt with another patient, a visit from a close friend, an attentive and kindly doctor who has time for a personal remark or a compliment instead of talking "past" the patient—all these things are of infinite value. They may make all the difference in encouraging the patient to read and study, to dare to venture out among people, to start the long fight with the authorities, to take the first step into life—life outside the walls of the insti-tution.

8

How do you manage?

It seems to be generally accepted among a lot of people that physically disabled people are sexually incompetent and destined to live without sexual pleasure. Of course there are injuries and illnesses which affect the sexual functions, for instance certain spine injuries, but experience has shown that the majority of physically disabled men can still have an erection. Ejaculation and orgasm are also quite possible. Even if sexual desires diminish and there is no hope of satisfaction, it may still be possible to have a sexual relationship with another person.Vilhelm Ekensteen, the Swedish author who is himself physically handicapped, writes in his book that there does not seem to be a handicap severe enough for there not to be room for some sexual activity. I agree. However much we are cut off or sheltered from sexual stimuli, however paralysed, deformed or amputated we are, our sexual needs are the same as other people's.

It is his healthy, natural sexual impulses which drive the institutionalized person to snatch a few moments of erotic pleasure in spite of humiliating rules and regulations, not dirty, unsound tendencies which, according to the authorities, must be stifled. Not even those who are totally paralysed and whose sensory nerves no longer function need to live in a de-sexualized limbo on the borderline between life and death. There are many examples of sexual relationships which have been started or continued after one of the partners has become disabled.

A friend of mine broke his neck some years ago in a car accident. He was an attractive man in his early thirties who loved fast cars and women. He was so badly injured that the doctors considered it useless to send him to a rehabilitation centre. Instead, his parents arranged a room for him in their home. He lay in bed all day staring at the ceiling, refusing to see all visitors. One of his girlfriends, however, was stubborn and insisted on seeing him. After some time, almost without knowing how it happened, they began a sexual relationship. They had discovered that he was capable of a reflex erection and if she was very active during intercourse, he could sustain it until she had an orgasm. He could feel nothing himself, but he was happy in the knowledge that he could still have a sexual relationship with a girl and make her happy too. The psychological satisfaction he derived and the joy and beauty of the act itself compensated him for his own lack of sexual release.

There are men who find it difficult to accept the passive role after becoming disabled. The handicapped woman does not always have the same difficulties. In our Western culture we believe that it is the male who must be the active partner and the one who makes the initial advances. It is not unusual to hear of women who are perfectly healthy and declare themselves quite satisfied although they have never reached an orgasm. For them the most important aspect of their sexual life is to satisfy their husband, they have come to terms with the completely passive role.

Men, on the other hand, have all the symbols of manhood and virility to keep up with, all the fictitious male figures of supreme sexual prowess who stride so confidently across the film and TV screens and pose magnificently on every page in the glossy magazines. No wonder that so many disabled men feel terrified at the thought of returning to a normal married life when all their healthy lives

47

they have striven to live up to these false images. For some men the physical handicap may even come as a relief, they no longer have to compete, they can withdraw honourably from the artificial competition.

Many marriages fail when one partner becomes physically disabled. In some cases sexual life is completely discontinued and the marriage continues on the basis that the helpless invalid satisfies other needs in the partner, the need to be a martyr or a mother figure, for instance, or because of a sense of duty. But the handicap can also be the beginning of a freer, deeper relationship than before.

"Do you get angry with your body?" a friend once asked me. Yes, it does happen that I feel angry with my immovable legs and my silly hands which can't grip properly, and annoyed with myself for not being able to function sexually anywhere but in bed, not being able to improvise and make love wherever or however I want to. But there are many ways of overcoming the difficulties caused by a physical disablement, intuitive short cuts to the greatest amount of pleasure, so long as there is enough love and understanding. Many times the partners are forced to adopt more relaxed and abandoned attitudes, to experiment with positions which could perhaps serve even the able-bodied well if their sexual life has become unadventurous and monotonous. There is the satisfaction of oral love or of experiments with mechanical aids which may sometimes give as great or greater satisfaction than ordinary intercourse, for when the inter-relation between two people is based on mutual love and respect nothing is wrong or "sinful".

Sometimes the wish to experiment can appear quite shocking to oneself and suspicions that one is a sexual deviant may result: am I abnormal, is what I am doing wrong? Would it not be better to submit to my fate in case people were to suspect my actions? It is easy for intense feelings of guilt to begin to develop. This is why I feel it is so important for people to understand that everything which increases sexual joy is permissible as long as it does not cause physical or mental pain to either of the partners. Besides, our fantasies and actions are probably never quite as unique as we imagine. Perhaps there is a special need of extra erotic stimulation for the physically handicapped person before he can enjoy his sexual potential to the full. But sex is still fun for the disabled—it is a source of joy and happiness in an otherwise dreary and monotonous existence.

Sometimes it may be too difficult for the man who is concerned about his prestige, or for the woman filled with inhibitions, to change his or her technique in bed because one of the partners has become disabled. They may feel that it is easier to abandon sexual pleasure altogether than to change their precious habits—but their sexual needs will still be there beneath the surface, aching, demanding.

It would be of great help to people finding themselves in such situations to have someone to discuss their problems with, a psychiatrist or a doctor at a rehabilitation centre with special emphasis on sexual problems. At the moment there are no such services and, taking into consideration the negative attitudes of most medical authorities and social counsellors, I can see it being a very long time before these needs are taken seriously. Even social organizations directly concerned with family relationships do not pay any special attention to these sexual problems. An important aspect of this help would be a changed attitude towards the roles of the sexes, a willingness to admit that the woman need not necessarily be a passive appendix to the active man—in bed or out of it. If people were brave enough to adopt different roles—and different positions in bed—the change would not be so radical and the mechanical aids would not seem so embarrassing and shocking when tragedy strikes.

But there is also the psychological aspect of sexuality. To be able to retain one's sexual capacity is of enormous psychological importance to even the most severely disabled person. A young man I know who had broken his neck in a diving accident was offered an operation which would relieve him of painful spasms and bladder trouble. At first he gratefully accepted the suggestion, but when he learned that he would lose his capacity to have an erection in the future, he categorically refused. It was psychologically more important to him to retain his sexual capacity, although he was almost totally paralysed, than to be relieved of his physical pains.

I feel it is about time that we leave off thinking that sex is something exclusively for the whole and the healthy. It is no longer possible to draw up boundaries for those who are allowed to join in and those who are not—it is time for the sexual needs of everybody to be accepted.

The physically handicapped—a sexual minority?

During the last years a lot of attention has been paid to sexual minorities and many books have been written on the subject exposing the humiliations and lack of understanding suffered by those who are different. The physically disabled are regarded in some quarters as belonging to the sexual minorities. In the film *From the Language of Love*, a short, delicate love scene between two physically handicapped people was shown. It was put there almost as an afterthought between the various professional performances of sexually deviant couples. Personally I question the tendency to include the physically disabled among sexual minority groups. It seems to me wrong, to begin with, to treat the physically handicapped as a homogeneous group, as they consist, on the whole, of a cross-section of the community which has been struck down by illness or accidental injury and among whom the same percentages of bisexual, homosexual and sexually deviant persons are likely to be found as amongst the rest of the population. It is important to emphasize that the sexual behaviour pattern of the physically handicapped is largely the same as that of the rest of the population.

The problems of the handicapped are not, however, going to be solved by sanctioning heterosexual relationships alone, but a new liberal attitude, which would include the physically disabled person's right to a homosexual relationship without fear or shame or anxiety, is also needed.

The majority of physically handicapped persons are heterosexual and many of them have satisfactory sexual relationships with a member of the opposite sex. Many more long for such a relationship. These people do not belong to a sexual minority group but they need help in order to function sexually. This help, if given, ought also to be given to bisexuals and homosexuals. The sexually deviant among the physically disabled have a heavy burden to carry, theirs is a double handicap.

9

Interviews and so-called authorities

A physically disabled person is often regarded as peculiar, a strange phenomenon, a queer bird whose handicap and deviant behaviour sometimes appears to the healthy on-looker as an invitation to trespass on the sick person's private ground. People feel entitled to ask the sort of questions they would never normally ask: "Can you feel? Are you really married?" There is a reluctance to answer, a shyness to return the question and thereby remove its sting.

"Do you sleep with your husband?" Most handicapped people would regard questions of that kind humiliating. We feel exposed and embarrassed and don't know how to behave or what to say. None of us have had all that much training in the technique of establishing relationships with the able-bodied members of society. It is not so easy to be "with it" and join in while still feeling isolated. We hardly ever meet anybody but our own kind. Perhaps the question was quite innocently posed, perhaps it could have become a first step towards further contact—always provided that some sort of communication could have been established at all and the disabled person had not been feeling too much like a stranger on a visit to the land of the healthy.

As a rule, though, it isn't only inquisitiveness which makes the able-bodied person ask about the sex life of the physically disabled, but the surprise of suddenly finding himself confronted by somebody paralysed. "How on earth does she manage? Can she really function properly?"

These sort of questions would be unnecessary if some kind of education about handicapped people existed in schools. As it is, those who are genuinely interested have to walk the tightrope between their own prejudices and the fears the disabled have of being regarded as abnormal.

"So you do enjoy sleeping with your husband—that's fine."

This kind of talk may sometimes be a way of overcoming prejudices and may lead to further and more intimate talks, it may present an opportunity to discuss the humiliations we suffer, our need for equality. The reaction may often take the form of an astonished exclamation: "Good God, and we always thought that conditions were so perfect for the physically handicapped in the Welfare State! What on earth do we pay taxes for if those who already suffer so much are made to live like that?"

At the same time the handicapped are afforded insight into the world of the able-bodied. It makes us realize that everything is not perfect simply because a person can walk, that sexual problems exist even if one is strong and healthy, that to be able to move freely does not mean having sexual intercourse every night! A dialogue is established, perhaps a growing friendship or, at least, an opportunity to make contact—all too important to be lost through evasion or shyness.

The so called experts who, following a pattern set by some countries abroad, are investigating the sexual problems of the physically disabled in Sweden, often complain about the wall of silence they come up against when they attempt personal interviews with the disabled about the existence—or non-existence—of their sexual life. The silence in this case is easily understood. They are the same medical experts who have objected when tender love affairs have been discovered.

In an institution you live in an impersonal milieu without even a corner to yourself, you are allowed only a few personal belongings, some photographs, various toilet articles. The staff enter the room which you are often forced to share with others without knocking on the door —which of course has no lock—doctors and other "experts" talk above your head about you, but only as a case, never as a person; your economic circumstances are most likely poor, hospitalization is a dreaded reality, and your spiritual life is practically non-existent. If your arms are reasonably movable, you masturbate until your soul smarts and the loneliness you experience afterwards is not something you feel particularly willing to talk about to somebody compiling statistics. You grow weary of interviews which never lead to improvements, interviews which treat your deepest, most personal dreams and traumas in a depersonalized, coldly statistical way.

I can't refrain from asking myself: why is it that the experts have suddenly become interested in the sexual activities of the physically disabled? Why are so many statistical tables concerning the effect of different forms of disablement on sexual capacity being prepared? Why are questions asked about sexual education in schools for physically disabled children and young people? Is it because of a real concern for the disabled, a genuine wish that we should at last be allowed our sexual freedom? Or is it because this is a new and hitherto unworked field which can afford the investigators great distinctions?

I don't know the answer. But the fact is that in spite of epoch-making American investigations into the sexual potency of men with severe spinal disabilities (which incidentally were found to be astonishingly high) carried out as early as the 1950s in Sweden—a country generally regarded as sexually progressive—sexual activity is still repressed within all hospitals and rehabilitation centres.

The most important measures needed now, if the sexual conditions of the disabled are to be improved, are radical attempts to change the attitudes of both staff and authorities of our nursing institutions. This is where I feel the "experts" have failed us. Their researches and investigations should be part of the "action for the disabled", not specialized reading for the initiated. But to insist on changed attitudes would perhaps not be profitable for the "experts". On the other hand, the results they may expose could quite possibly cause a stir in medical journals the world over.

When I wanted to do some interviewing myself in connection with writing this book, I was told by many people that I would be attempting an impossible task. But everywhere I went I found everyone to be most friendly, both the disabled and the nursing staff. The interviews often became long intimate talks about mutual problems and we asked each other questions—we were, after all, in the same boat—and we soon found that we could give each other constructive suggestions and ideas. Most of the disabled had never before been able to discuss their sexual problems in a serious way and they all agreed that it was of paramount importance to share them with someone in the same situation. All that was needed was a willingness on both sides to be frank and open and not just to expect the other one to do all the talking.

None of the twenty or so disabled to whom I talked had ever had a positive sexual experience in satisfying conditions inside a hospital or an institution. Even the most innocent incidents were regarded with suspicion by the staff. One young girl, for instance, told me how she had fallen in love with a young boy in one of the sanatoriums on the coast. He was able to walk fairly well and liked to take her for a walk in her wheelchair round the hospital garden before she had to go to bed at seven o'clock in the evening. One evening they got back ten minutes late; they were forbidden to take any further walks together. Nobody showed any understanding of their youth and their first tender sexual explorations. Neither of them had anyone to turn to for help, the women who shared the girl's room were on average forty years older than she was and themselves living in complete isolation.

I didn't find that those living outside the institutions felt any sexually freer. One boy said: "If your legs are handicapped, people think your head is handicapped too."

One woman, whose husband had divorced her and who lived alone in a small flat, didn't dare to buy herself a mechanical aid because of her home help. She was afraid that the home help might think her "dirty" and perhaps report her to the hospital authorities, or leave her if she found the aid. There was some reason for this anxiety as the home help had already pronounced disapproval of a slightly erotic painting in the bedroom.

In my opinion, the only way to change these humiliating conditions is for us to talk openly about our experiences and difficulties without consulting the authorities. There is no reason for us to protect from publicity those who, in our opinion, have infringed on our freedom so mercilessly; on the contrary, it is our duty to name them. We mustn't let ourselves be frightened by anonymous authorities any more. We disabled can form discussion groups and study groups where we can voice our opinions. I believe that we are the best judges of how our own problems can be solved. We are the ones with the experience, we are the real authorities. It is we who have had to suffer the humiliations of having to steal moments of guilty sex during the long years of hospitalization. It is up to us to make suggestions and to force the authorities to help us implement them.

10

The right to love

Few people are forced to expose themselves in the nude so often as the physically disabled who can't look after their own hygiene. Depersonalized into organic bundles, their bodies and private parts are washed. Erotic fantasies whirl around in the head like overheated spinning-tops when the nurse touches the erogenous zones between the legs or gives an enema. Your private parts are as depersonalized as yourself, they are washed and cleaned in a way regarded as natural for sick people; perhaps it is right, but the sexually deprived are forced to lie there exposed with expressionless faces hoping that no one will notice what pleasure or disgust they are experiencing. It is especially degrading for men to be aroused, time and time again, to an unbearable point, only to be left in the certain knowledge that it will never be different than this.

You feel lonely—lonely and sexy and sad. Incarcerated in the hospital rooms without pictures on the walls, in the half-light seeping through drawn curtains, the lifelong patients live out their slow day's journey into night. In the oppressive silence, glued to their beds, they lose their identity, isolation and loneliness break down their emotional life, they sink into a silent, passive stupor. The ability to concentrate diminishes, they turn the pages of a magazine absentmindedly or sit and gaze at a pin-up which a well-meaning nurse has pinned to the wardrobe door.

Sexual desires flash through your body but anguish and

fear for what "they" will think conquer, you sink back into silence and stillness. There is a smell of over-ripe pears in the room. In the next bed the patient moans. You haven't the strength to weep. You just want to be gone. The words of the Swedish poet Stagnelius about our endless capacity to demand and the necessity to sacrifice become a living reality.

Sometimes the result of this inner conflict expresses itself in a "false" self which appears to have adapted splendidly to the anti-sexual attitude of the hospital. But it is impossible to pull up sexual impulse by the roots, and for those who are immobile there are few opportunities to sublimate the sexual drive into other activities. There are few chances of fruitful political or religious activities, no practical opportunities to engage in meaningful artistic work, little possibility of enriching one's everyday life.

Many people would agree that it is unreasonable to deprive the physically disabled of all possibilities of having a private life. The privilege of a locked door has not yet reached the institutions, you are regarded as public property in a way which almost compares with enforced prostitution. Visitors walk in and out through the room, new nurses turn up to help with one's most intimate hygiene without as much as introducing themselves, the doctor glides past on his rounds without saying a word— it's enough to make one want to stick one's tongue out to see if he is capable of any reaction at all!

The doctors are only too well aware of the sexually impoverished world in which the long-term patients have to exist. But instead of trying to help create a more positive milieu for these people to meet their loved ones in, they hide behind their blinkers in an effort to deny all knowledge of the patient's sexual misery.

One of the worst features of this is that there is nowhere for the patient to go with her or his friend. It is humiliating to have to hide in cupboards or crawl into culverts like dying elephants—embarrassing to have to ask friends to stand watch by the door, as if one were committing a burglary. There are no rooms for lovers to be in, no guest apartments for visiting families to stay in. Man and wife can no longer share a bed when one of them is physically disabled for life. The choice is either a life of celibacy or of faithlessness for the able-bodied partner for whom the door of the institution is always open. He or she can take all that the world outside offers, and you need a strong character indeed not to fall for the temptations which beset you in your loneliness after the short visiting hour.

A girl in a home had been courageous enough to buy a mechanical aid, a vibrator, by post. In spite of partial paralysis of the arms she had found a way of satisfying herself when she went to the lavatory, the only place in the hospital, needless to say, which had a key in the door, and where she had a natural reason to ask for help with her underclothes. The vibrator produced a high note which could be heard in the corridor. On one occasion the sound was heard by the sister, who immediately demanded that the door be opened—and there the girl sat, exposed in her misery and degradation. The vibrator was removed and would only be returned if the patient ever left the hospital.

Anyone who has stayed any time in an institution knows only too well that painful scenes like this often happen, and that it very seldom occurs that a nurse or a sister turns a blind eye to any kind of sexual activity.

A beautiful young student who had worked as a go-go girl contracted multiple sclerosis and grew worse and worse. After a year she was confined to a wheelchair and became extremely depressed. She regarded her ability to attract men as totally lost and this caused her intense suffering. After a few years she ended up in an institution where she met a young patient who fell in love with her.

She was pleased about the attention and tenderness he showed her and they became lovers. There was nowhere else for them to be alone except in her room so they decided to take her room-mates into their confidence rather than risk being interrupted by them. The room-mates were all on their side, they even acted as guards for the lovers and all went well without any unpleasant disturbance.

Next morning two nurses discovered a spot of sperm on the sheets. The young couple, both in their mid-twenties, were called before the doctor of the ward and thoroughly interrogated. They were forbidden to meet again. The girl, who was regarded as oversexed, perhaps because of her previous profession, was given permission to use a mechanical aid, but was forbidden to mention it to the other patients as there could be no question of allowing it generally.

It seems to me that the sexual problems in hospitals and institutions are not insoluble. All that is needed is a private room with a key and the right to be alone with a visitor, whether one wants to make love or not. What takes place in private and who the patient wishes to mix with is surely his own business.

If a visitor has come a long way and wishes to spend a night, it ought to be possible to rent a small flat within the hospital. The flat could easily be fitted with a small cooker for making tea or cooking simple meals, a sitting-room in warm, friendly colours, perhaps with a radio or a record-player, and a bedroom designed for handicapped people.

It would be wrong to label it a "sex room". There are many disabled people who would simply like to meet a friend in privacy. It is important, too, that a small rent should be charged for a flat like that in order that the handicapped patient may feel quite independent and fully within his rights to do what he wants.

It is not often that two severely handicapped people fall

in love with each other, but when it does happen it is important that they should be given every opportunity to express their love sexually. Although sex is fundamentally an activity between two people, there may be occasions when the partners are so gravely handicapped that they need the assistance of a third person. But for many paralysed people who can no longer experience feelings, it may be enough just to share a room with the loved one, to lie close together and touch those parts of each other's bodies that can still respond to touch, to be alone together—to talk about love.

In reality, the physically disabled of different sexes are prevented from sharing a room in hospitals. The separation of male and female has become so ingrained in some hospital authorities that not even married couples are allowed in the same room. An incident which took place in a famous Swedish rehabilitation centre illustrates the abhorrence felt at the thought of the physically disabled wanting to lead a normal life. An engaged couple in their twenties asked to be allowed to share a room but were refused on the grounds that the matron had threatened to leave if their request was granted. She openly declared that she found the thought of handicapped people of different sexes living together intolerable.

But there are some among the nursing staff who take a different view. In spite of it being forbidden for two disabled people to spend their free weekends together, it sometimes happens that a nurse will help to book a room in an hotel for them, or buy a "girlie" magazine for a patient. Sometimes it happens too that one of the domestics will work overtime to enable two lovers to spend a few more moments together before being parted at bedtime.

But those who understand are a small minority. Others are afraid of losing their jobs if they are too helpful, this applies particularly to homes hidden away in the depths of the countryside, perhaps the only place for miles around that offers part-time jobs to women.

In some hospitals and institutions both staff and patients appear to be convinced that it is unlawful for them to have intimate relationships. This is a myth, probably created by the anti-sexual attitudes of matrons and doctors. The belief that a staff member can be dismissed without a reference if he is discovered having a sexual relationship with a patient is actually quite unfounded. The only existing law is one which protects the patients from being sexually interfered with by the nursing staff. There is no law against a mutually agreed relationship. The fact that the age limit at which a physically disabled person is legally permitted to have sexual intercourse is eighteen as opposed to the normal fifteen, is another indication that the authorities do not consider us responsible for our own actions. Other countries are not so backward—in Britain, for instance, the age of consent to sexual intercourse is sixteen for everybody.

All the same it sometimes happens that one of the staff has a relationship with one of the patients, usually young girls who fall in love with young men injured in traffic or diving accidents. The fact that these relationships sometimes end in marriage proves that they are founded on love and not just pity.

Strong forces are at work for the preservation of institutions. Instead of liberalizing and modifying the existing ones, a completely new concept of non-institutionalized home-service is needed. This would also have the advantage of being cheaper in the long run. Many people would like to see the physically disabled remain in institutions and more educational organizations, study groups, etc., allowed to provide interest and occupation for the patients. This seems to me the most dangerous attitude of all, a way of preserving for ever the establishment's view of institutions.

62

We would no longer be looked upon as "sick" people, just prisoners for life because society happens to regard hospitals and institutions as convenient places in which to keep their physically disabled for ever. It seems to me far more important to give us a chance to live in the world and to give us the freedom to attend as many educational organizations and study groups as we like—wherever and whenever we like!

These last years there have been several suggestions that so-called "sexual samaritans" should be employed for the physically handicapped confined in institutions. It is often suggested by well-meaning radical people who believe that they have the welfare of the disabled at heart. But in reality it would only help to entrench the already existing prejudices in institutions and restrict even further the patient's chances of becoming integrated into society. One can hear people say: "What on earth do they want to come out for? They have got everything in there!"

Of course there are many sexually frustrated, disabled persons who are imprisoned in institutions, hospitals or in their own homes; but is it likely that they, who have been indoctrinated from childhood to look at themselves as sexual outsiders, would ever be able to regard a State- or hospital-run sexual "service" as anything but shameful? The idea that our nursing institutions should provide such a service seems absurd to me, not for moral reasons, but because of my personal experience of the artificial, authoritarian world of the hospital which makes it only too obvious how this service would function: "Right, Mr. Smith, sexual service on Thursday between three and four." There would be no personal initiative from the patient, no contact with the "samaritan" except through a data machine, forms—in triplicate—would have to be filled in stating exact time, date and place three weeks before the required service, the requests would be carefully investigated and finally sanctioned by the medical authorities, the strictest control over hygiene and sterilized instruments would be instituted and the only personal freedom left to the patient would be the freedom to say : no, thank you!

In a society geared to helping the physically disabled we would be able to solve our sexual problems ourselves. The problems are very much the same as other people's; the prettiest, most attractive and most intelligent ones are successful in finding a partner while for less attractive and inhibited people it is more difficult. This we share with the able-bodied, but there is a difference : a lonely, severely disabled person is not even capable of masturbating and relieving himself of painfully recurring sexual pressures. There is a real need for light, mechanical aids to masturbation, so constructed that even the most severely disabled person can use them alone.

In the outside world—if you are a man and you have enough money—you can buy "love" from a prostitute. This is a personal thing and quite different from having a "service" laid on by a State-run organization. It is sad that some people can only achieve sexual satisfaction through the degradation of another, but it can hardly be expected that the physically handicapped of this world should lead the fight against prostitution. As long as prostitution exists, the physically disabled must be allowed to avail themselves of it, even if they are living in institutions. Society has no right to demand higher moral standards from them than from anybody else. They must be allowed to choose; this is the basis of all moral actions and the only way through which a changed attitude towards them will be achieved.

By these arguments I appear to be pleading for better conditions in the institutions when all the time my argument has been that they should be abolished. However, I know only too well that it will be a very long time before they are; and until then the physically disabled will go on being imprisoned in institutions, and as long as they are, I will go on pleading for better conditions.

We may have to wait, but while we wait, we must be allowed to love.